The Dim Sum Cookbook

More Than 50 Mouth-Watering Dim Sum Recipes

BY: Ivy Hope

Copyright/License Page

Table of Contents

Introduction

There nothing is more tempting than a delicious Asian Dim Sum. Rolled, stuffed, sealed and steamed. Asian Dim Sums are also unexpectedly very easy to cook and eaten at home. This recipe book offers 50 delicious and simple recipes.

The unique ability of these recipes is that they interpret authentic Asian cooking techniques for Western cooks. The easy to understand recipes for Asia's popular savory or sweet little parcels, pockets, packs, and desserts range from chicken to succulent pork dim-sum and from mushy cherry to juicy pineapple dim-sum.

These Dim Sum recipes cover East, South-east, and South Asia, with recipes from all parts of Asia. Throughout the recipe book only the best technique for shaping, stuffing, steaming, and serving each kind of dim-sums is offered.

It's pretty easy to include dim-sums into your meals with a thorough explanation to requisite equipment and ingredients and servings with time-saving shortcuts, which yield delightful results.

Become a dim-sum master with the help of experts. Making mouth-watering, innovative dim-sums has never been simpler to make with most desired recipes and methods.

Every recipe in this cookbook will help you create unique dim-sums that will amaze your family as well as friends.

Boiled Chicken Dim Sum

Dim Sums with boiled chicken and cabbage!

Serves: 2

Preparation Time: 30 minutes

Cooking Time: 15 minutes

Ingredients

For Dough

- 1/8 teaspoon salt
- 1 1/2 cups flour
- water for kneading

For Filling

- 1/2 tablespoon dark soy sauce
- 1/2 tablespoon white vinegar
- 1 cup boiled chicken, minced
- 1 tablespoon peanut oil
- 1 small onion, finely minced
- 1 cup cabbage, finely chopped
- 1 teaspoon garlic paste

Method

1. For dough, combine salt and flour in a bowl. Add in water gradually to make dough. Knead the dough into a bowl and set aside for half an hour.

2. For filling, combine all ingredients for filling and mix well.

3. Now. make 30 balls out of prepared dough and roll each one of them into 3 inches circle.

4. Then, place one of the rolled ball over a dim-sum mould and place 2 teaspoons of prepared filling in the centre. Apply some water at the edges and fold the mould into half to seal the dim-sum

5. Use the same method and rest of the dim-sums.

6. Line up a steam basket with cabbage leaves and place the prepared dim-sums in it. Then place the basket over boiling water and cook for 10-15 minutes or until done.

7. Serve hot with soy sauce!

Carrot Dim Sum

Dim Sums with carrot and cabbage filling!

Serves: 2

Preparation Time: 30 minutes

Cooking Time: 15 minutes

Ingredients

For Dough

- 1/8 teaspoon salt
- 1 1/2 cups flour
- water for kneading

For Filling

- 1/2 tablespoon dark soy sauce
- 1/2 tablespoon white vinegar
- 1 cup carrots, grated
- 1 tablespoon peanut oil
- 1 small onion, finely minced
- 1 cup cabbage, finely chopped
- 1 teaspoon garlic paste

Method

1. For dough, combine salt and flour in a bowl. Add in water gradually to make dough. Knead the dough into a bowl and set aside for half an hour.

2. For filling, combine all ingredients for filling and mix well.

3. Now. make 30 balls out of prepared dough and roll each one of them into 3 inches circle.

4. Then, place one of the rolled ball over a dim-sum mould and place 2 teaspoons of prepared filling in the centre. Apply some water at the edges and fold the mould into half to seal the dim-sum

5. Use the same method and rest of the dim-sums.

6. Line up a steam basket with cabbage leaves and place the prepared dim-sums in it. Then place the basket over boiling water and cook for 10-15 minutes or until done.

7. Serve hot with soy sauce!

Cabbage Dim Sum

Dim Sums with boiled onion and cabbage filling!

Serves: 2

Preparation Time: 30 minutes

Cooking Time: 15 minutes

Ingredients

For Dough

- 1/8 teaspoon salt
- 1 1/2 cups flour
- water for kneading

For Filling

- 1/2 tablespoon dark soy sauce
- 1/2 tablespoon white vinegar
- 1 tablespoon peanut oil
- 1 large onion, finely minced
- 1 1/2 cups cabbage, finely chopped
- 1 teaspoon garlic paste

Method

1. For dough, combine salt and flour in a bowl. Add in water gradually to make dough. Knead the dough into a bowl and set aside for half an hour.

2. For filling, combine all ingredients for filling and mix well.

3. Now. make 30 balls out of prepared dough and roll each one of them into 3 inches circle.

4. Then, place one of the rolled ball over a dim-sum mould and place 2 teaspoons of prepared filling in the centre. Apply some water at the edges and fold the mould into half to seal the dim-sum

5. Use the same method and rest of the dim-sums.

6. Line up a steam basket with cabbage leaves and place the prepared dim-sums in it. Then place the basket over boiling water and cook for 10-15 minutes or until done.

7. Serve hot with soy sauce!

Cherry Dim Sum

Dim Sums with cherry jam filling!

Serves: 2

Preparation Time: 30 minutes

Cooking Time: 15 minutes

Ingredients

For Dough

- 1/8 teaspoon salt
- 1 1/2 cups flour
- water for kneading

For Filling

- 2 cups cherry jam

Method

1. For dough, combine salt and flour in a bowl. Add in water gradually to make dough. Knead the dough into a bowl and set aside for half an hour.

2. Now. make 30 balls out of prepared dough and roll each one of them into 3 inches circle.

3. Then, place one of the rolled ball over a dim-sum mould and place 2 teaspoons of filling in the centre. Apply some water at the edges and fold the mould into half to seal the dim-sum

4. Use the same method and rest of the dim-sums.

5. Line up a steam basket with cabbage leaves and place the prepared dim-sums in it. Then place the basket over boiling water and cook for 10-15 minutes or until done.

6. Serve hot with soy sauce!

Potato Dim Sum

Dim Sums with boiled potatoes and cabbage!

Serves: 2

Preparation Time: 30 minutes

Cooking Time: 15 minutes

Ingredients

For Dough

- 1/8 teaspoon salt
- 1 1/2 cups flour
- water for kneading

For Filling

- 1/2 tablespoon dark soy sauce
- 1/2 tablespoon white vinegar
- 1 cup boiled potatoes, mashed
- 1 tablespoon peanut oil
- 1 small onion, finely minced
- 1 cup cabbage, finely chopped
- 1 teaspoon garlic paste

Method

1. For dough, combine salt and flour in a bowl. Add in water gradually to make dough. Knead the dough into a bowl and set aside for half an hour.

2. For filling, combine all ingredients for filling and mix well.

3. Now. make 30 balls out of prepared dough and roll each one of them into 3 inches circle.

4. Then, place one of the rolled ball over a dim-sum mould and place 2 teaspoons of prepared filling in the centre. Apply some water at the edges and fold the mould into half to seal the dim-sum

5. Use the same method and rest of the dim-sums.

6. Line up a steam basket with cabbage leaves and place the prepared dim-sums in it. Then place the basket over boiling water and cook for 10-15 minutes or until done.

7. Serve hot with soy sauce!

Tandoori Chicken Dim Sum

Dim Sums with tandoori chicken and cabbage!

Serves: 2

Preparation Time: 30 minutes

Cooking Time: 15 minutes

Ingredients

For Dough

- 1/8 teaspoon salt
- 1 1/2 cups flour
- water for kneading

For Filling

- 1/2 tablespoon dark soy sauce
- 1/2 tablespoon white vinegar
- 1 cup tandoori chicken, shredded
- 1 tablespoon peanut oil
- 1 small onion, finely minced
- 1 cup cabbage, finely chopped
- 1 teaspoon garlic paste

Method

1. For dough, combine salt and flour in a bowl. Add in water gradually to make dough. Knead the dough into a bowl and set aside for half an hour.

2. For filling, combine all ingredients for filling and mix well.

3. Now. make 30 balls out of prepared dough and roll each one of them into 3 inches circle.

4. Then, place one of the rolled ball over a dim-sum mould and place 2 teaspoons of prepared filling in the centre. Apply some water at the edges and fold the mould into half to seal the dim-sum

5. Use the same method and rest of the dim-sums.

6. Line up a steam basket with cabbage leaves and place the prepared dim-sums in it. Then place the basket over boiling water and cook for 10-15 minutes or until done.

7. Serve hot with soy sauce!

Feta Dim Sum

Dim Sums with feta cheese and cabbage!

Serves: 2

Preparation Time: 30 minutes

Cooking Time: 15 minutes

Ingredients

For Dough

- 1/8 teaspoon salt
- 1 1/2 cups flour
- water for kneading

For Filling

- 1/2 tablespoon dark soy sauce
- 1/2 tablespoon white vinegar
- 1 cup feta cheese, crumpled
- 1 tablespoon peanut oil
- 1 small onion, finely minced
- 1 cup cabbage, finely chopped
- 1 teaspoon garlic paste

Method

1. For dough, combine salt and flour in a bowl. Add in water gradually to make dough. Knead the dough into a bowl and set aside for half an hour.

2. For filling, combine all ingredients for filling and mix well.

3. Now. make 30 balls out of prepared dough and roll each one of them into 3 inches circle.

4. Then, place one of the rolled ball over a dim-sum mould and place 2 teaspoons of prepared filling in the centre. Apply some water at the edges and fold the mould into half to seal the dim-sum

5. Use the same method and rest of the dim-sums.

6. Line up a steam basket with cabbage leaves and place the prepared dim-sums in it. Then place the basket over boiling water and cook for 10-15 minutes or until done.

7. Serve hot with soy sauce!

Pineapple Dim Sum

Dim Sums with pineapple jam filling!

Serves: 2

Preparation Time: 30 minutes

Cooking Time: 15 minutes

Ingredients

For Dough

- 1/8 teaspoon salt
- 1 1/2 cups flour
- water for kneading

For Filling

- 2 cups pineapple jam

Method

1. For dough, combine salt and flour in a bowl. Add in water gradually to make dough. Knead the dough into a bowl and set aside for half an hour.

2. Now. make 30 balls out of prepared dough and roll each one of them into 3 inches circle.

3. Then, place one of the rolled ball over a dim-sum mould and place 2 teaspoons of filling in the centre. Apply some water at the edges and fold the mould into half to seal the dim-sum

4. Use the same method and rest of the dim-sums.

5. Line up a steam basket with cabbage leaves and place the prepared dim-sums in it. Then place the basket over boiling water and cook for 10-15 minutes or until done.

6. Serve hot with soy sauce!

Cauliflower Dim Sum

Dim Sums with cauliflower and cabbage!

Serves: 2

Preparation Time: 30 minutes

Cooking Time: 15 minutes

Ingredients

For Dough

- 1/8 teaspoon salt
- 1 1/2 cups flour
- water for kneading

For Filling

- 1/2 tablespoon dark soy sauce
- 1/2 tablespoon white vinegar
- 1 cup cauliflower, grated
- 1 tablespoon peanut oil
- 1 small onion, finely minced
- 1 cup cabbage, finely chopped
- 1 teaspoon garlic paste

Method

1. For dough, combine salt and flour in a bowl. Add in water gradually to make dough. Knead the dough into a bowl and set aside for half an hour.

2. For filling, combine all ingredients for filling and mix well.

3. Now. make 30 balls out of prepared dough and roll each one of them into 3 inches circle.

4. Then, place one of the rolled ball over a dim-sum mould and place 2 teaspoons of prepared filling in the centre. Apply some water at the edges and fold the mould into half to seal the dim-sum

5. Use the same method and rest of the dim-sums.

6. Line up a steam basket with cabbage leaves and place the prepared dim-sums in it. Then place the basket over boiling water and cook for 10-15 minutes or until done.

7. Serve hot with soy sauce!

Minced Beef Dim Sum

Dim Sums with minced beef and cabbage!

Serves: 2

Preparation Time: 30 minutes

Cooking Time: 15 minutes

Ingredients

For Dough

- 1/8 teaspoon salt
- 1 1/2 cups flour
- water for kneading

For Filling

- 1/2 tablespoon dark soy sauce
- 1/2 tablespoon white vinegar
- 1 cup minced beef
- 1 tablespoon peanut oil
- 1 small onion, finely minced
- 1 cup cabbage, finely chopped
- 1 teaspoon garlic paste

Method

1. For dough, combine salt and flour in a bowl. Add in water gradually to make dough. Knead the dough into a bowl and set aside for half an hour.

2. For filling, combine all ingredients for filling and mix well.

3. Now. make 30 balls out of prepared dough and roll each one of them into 3 inches circle.

4. Then, place one of the rolled ball over a dim-sum mould and place 2 teaspoons of prepared filling in the centre. Apply some water at the edges and fold the mould into half to seal the dim-sum

5. Use the same method and rest of the dim-sums.

6. Line up a steam basket with cabbage leaves and place the prepared dim-sums in it. Then place the basket over boiling water and cook for 10-15 minutes or until done.

7. Serve hot with soy sauce!

Kabab Dim Sum

Dim Sums with crumpled kababs and cabbage!

Serves: 2

Preparation Time: 30 minutes

Cooking Time: 15 minutes

Ingredients

For Dough

- 1/8 teaspoon salt
- 1 1/2 cups flour
- water for kneading

For Filling

- 1/2 tablespoon dark soy sauce
- 1/2 tablespoon white vinegar
- 1 cup kababs, crumpled
- 1 tablespoon peanut oil
- 1 small onion, finely minced
- 1 cup cabbage, finely chopped
- 1 teaspoon garlic paste

Method

1. For dough, combine salt and flour in a bowl. Add in water gradually to make dough. Knead the dough into a bowl and set aside for half an hour.

2. For filling, combine all ingredients for filling and mix well.

3. Now. make 30 balls out of prepared dough and roll each one of them into 3 inches circle.

4. Then, place one of the rolled ball over a dim-sum mould and place 2 teaspoons of prepared filling in the centre. Apply some water at the edges and fold the mould into half to seal the dim-sum

5. Use the same method and rest of the dim-sums.

6. Line up a steam basket with cabbage leaves and place the prepared dim-sums in it. Then place the basket over boiling water and cook for 10-15 minutes or until done.

7. Serve hot with soy sauce!

Apple Pie Dim Sum

Dim Sums with apple pie filling!

Serves: 2

Preparation Time: 30 minutes

Cooking Time: 15 minutes

Ingredients

For Dough

- 1/8 teaspoon salt
- 1 1/2 cups flour
- water for kneading

For Filling

- 2 cups apple pie filling

Method

1. For dough, combine salt and flour in a bowl. Add in water gradually to make dough. Knead the dough into a bowl and set aside for half an hour.

2. Now. make 30 balls out of prepared dough and roll each one of them into 3 inches circle.

3. Then, place one of the rolled ball over a dim-sum mould and place 2 teaspoons of filling in the centre. Apply some water at the edges and fold the mould into half to seal the dim-sum

4. Use the same method and rest of the dim-sums.

5. Line up a steam basket with cabbage leaves and place the prepared dim-sums in it. Then place the basket over boiling water and cook for 10-15 minutes or until done.

6. Serve hot with soy sauce!

Cinnamon Pecan Dim Sum

Dim Sums with pecans, honey and cinnamon filling!

Serves: 2

Preparation Time: 30 minutes

Cooking Time: 15 minutes

Ingredients

For Dough

- 1/8 teaspoon salt
- 1 1/2 cups flour
- water for kneading

For Filling

- 1/2 cup honey
- 1 1/2 cups pecans, finely chopped
- 1 teaspoon cinnamon powder

Method

1. For dough, combine salt and flour in a bowl. Add in water gradually to make dough. Knead the dough into a bowl and set aside for half an hour.

2. For filling, combine all ingredients for filling and mix well.

3. Now. make 30 balls out of prepared dough and roll each one of them into 3 inches circle.

4. Then, place one of the rolled ball over a dim-sum mould and place 2 teaspoons of prepared filling in the centre. Apply some water at the edges and fold the mould into half to seal the dim-sum

5. Use the same method and rest of the dim-sums.

6. Line up a steam basket with cabbage leaves and place the prepared dim-sums in it. Then place the basket over boiling water and cook for 10-15 minutes or until done.

7. Serve hot with soy sauce!

Onion Bell Pepper Dim Sum

Dim Sums with green bell pepper and onion!

Serves: 2

Preparation Time: 30 minutes

Cooking Time: 15 minutes

Ingredients

For Dough

- 1/8 teaspoon salt
- 1 1/2 cups flour
- water for kneading

For Filling

- 1/2 tablespoon dark soy sauce
- 1/2 tablespoon white vinegar
- 1 cup green bell pepper, finely chopped
- 1 tablespoon peanut oil
- 1 small onion, finely minced
- 1 cup cabbage, finely chopped
- 1 teaspoon garlic paste

Method

1. For dough, combine salt and flour in a bowl. Add in water gradually to make dough. Knead the dough into a bowl and set aside for half an hour.

2. For filling, combine all ingredients for filling and mix well.

3. Now. make 30 balls out of prepared dough and roll each one of them into 3 inches circle.

4. Then, place one of the rolled ball over a dim-sum mould and place 2 teaspoons of prepared filling in the centre. Apply some water at the edges and fold the mould into half to seal the dim-sum

5. Use the same method and rest of the dim-sums.

6. Line up a steam basket with cabbage leaves and place the prepared dim-sums in it. Then place the basket over boiling water and cook for 10-15 minutes or until done.

7. Serve hot with soy sauce!

Chowmein Dim Sum

Dim Sums with chow-mein!

Serves: 2

Preparation Time: 30 minutes

Cooking Time: 15 minutes

Ingredients

For Dough

- 1/8 teaspoon salt
- 1 1/2 cups flour
- water for kneading

For Filling

- 2 cups left over chow-mein, finely chopped

Method

1. For dough, combine salt and flour in a bowl. Add in water gradually to make dough. Knead the dough into a bowl and set aside for half an hour.

2. Now. make 30 balls out of prepared dough and roll each one of them into 3 inches circle.

3. Then, place one of the rolled ball over a dim-sum mould and place 2 teaspoons of filling in the centre. Apply some water at the edges and fold the mould into half to seal the dim-sum

4. Use the same method and rest of the dim-sums.

5. Line up a steam basket with cabbage leaves and place the prepared dim-sums in it. Then place the basket over boiling water and cook for 10-15 minutes or until done.

6. Serve hot with soy sauce!

Meat Ball Dim Sum

Dim Sums with mashed meat balls and cabbage!

Serves: 2

Preparation Time: 30 minutes

Cooking Time: 15 minutes

Ingredients

For Dough

- 1/8 teaspoon salt
- 1 1/2 cups flour
- water for kneading

For Filling

- 1/2 tablespoon dark soy sauce
- 1/2 tablespoon white vinegar
- 1 cup fried meat balls, mashed
- 1 tablespoon peanut oil
- 1 small onion, finely minced
- 1 cup cabbage, finely chopped
- 1 teaspoon garlic paste

Method

1. For dough, combine salt and flour in a bowl. Add in water gradually to make dough. Knead the dough into a bowl and set aside for half an hour.

2. For filling, combine all ingredients for filling and mix well.

3. Now. make 30 balls out of prepared dough and roll each one of them into 3 inches circle.

4. Then, place one of the rolled ball over a dim-sum mould and place 2 teaspoons of prepared filling in the centre. Apply some water at the edges and fold the mould into half to seal the dim-sum

5. Use the same method and rest of the dim-sums.

6. Line up a steam basket with cabbage leaves and place the prepared dim-sums in it. Then place the basket over boiling water and cook for 10-15 minutes or until done.

7. Serve hot with soy sauce

Turkey Dim Sum

Dim Sums with turkey and cabbage!

Serves: 2

Preparation Time: 30 minutes

Cooking Time: 15 minutes

Ingredients

For Dough

- 1/8 teaspoon salt
- 1 1/2 cups flour
- water for kneading

For Filling

- 1/2 tablespoon dark soy sauce
- 1/2 tablespoon white vinegar
- 1 cup turkey, minced
- 1 tablespoon peanut oil
- 1 small onion, finely minced
- 1 cup cabbage, finely chopped
- 1 teaspoon garlic paste

Method

1. For dough, combine salt and flour in a bowl. Add in water gradually to make dough. Knead the dough into a bowl and set aside for half an hour.

2. For filling, combine all ingredients for filling and mix well.

3. Now. make 30 balls out of prepared dough and roll each one of them into 3 inches circle.

4. Then, place one of the rolled ball over a dim-sum mould and place 2 teaspoons of prepared filling in the centre. Apply some water at the edges and fold the mould into half to seal the dim-sum

5. Use the same method and rest of the dim-sums.

6. Line up a steam basket with cabbage leaves and place the prepared dim-sums in it. Then place the basket over boiling water and cook for 10-15 minutes or until done.

7. Serve hot with soy sauce!

Chickpea Dim Sum

Dim Sums with boiled chickpeas and cabbage!

Serves: 2

Preparation Time: 30 minutes

Cooking Time: 15 minutes

Ingredients

For Dough

- 1/8 teaspoon salt
- 1 1/2 cups flour
- water for kneading

For Filling

- 1/2 tablespoon dark soy sauce
- 1/2 tablespoon white vinegar
- 1 cup boiled chickpeas, mashed
- 1 tablespoon peanut oil
- 1 small onion, finely minced
- 1 cup cabbage, finely chopped
- 1 teaspoon garlic paste

Method

1. For dough, combine salt and flour in a bowl. Add in water gradually to make dough. Knead the dough into a bowl and set aside for half an hour.

2. For filling, combine all ingredients for filling and mix well.

3. Now. make 30 balls out of prepared dough and roll each one of them into 3 inches circle.

4. Then, place one of the rolled ball over a dim-sum mould and place 2 teaspoons of prepared filling in the centre. Apply some water at the edges and fold the mould into half to seal the dim-sum

5. Use the same method and rest of the dim-sums.

6. Line up a steam basket with cabbage leaves and place the prepared dim-sums in it. Then place the basket over boiling water and cook for 10-15 minutes or until done.

7. Serve hot with soy sauce!

Corn Cheese Dim Sum

Dim Sums with corn kernels and mozzarella cheese!

Serves: 2

Preparation Time: 30 minutes

Cooking Time: 15 minutes

Ingredients

For Dough

- v1/8 teaspoon salt
- 1 1/2 cups flour
- water for kneading

For Filling

- 1/2 tablespoon dark soy sauce
- 1/2 tablespoon white vinegar
- 1 cup corn kernels
- 1/2 cup mozzarella cheese, grated
- 1 tablespoon peanut oil
- 1 small onion, finely minced
- 1 cup cabbage, finely chopped
- 1 teaspoon garlic paste

Method

1. For dough, combine salt and flour in a bowl. Add in water gradually to make dough. Knead the dough into a bowl and set aside for half an hour.

2. For filling, combine all ingredients for filling and mix well.

3. Now. make 30 balls out of prepared dough and roll each one of them into 3 inches circle.

4. Then, place one of the rolled ball over a dim-sum mould and place 2 teaspoons of prepared filling in the centre. Apply some water at the edges and fold the mould into half to seal the dim-sum

5. Use the same method and rest of the dim-sums.

6. Line up a steam basket with cabbage leaves and place the prepared dim-sums in it. Then place the basket over boiling water and cook for 10-15 minutes or until done.

7. Serve hot with soy sauce!

Tuna Dim Sum

Dim Sums with tuna flakes and cabbage!

Serves: 2

Preparation Time: 30 minutes

Cooking Time: 15 minutes

Ingredients

For Dough

- 1/8 teaspoon salt
- 1 1/2 cups flour
- water for kneading

For Filling

- 1/2 tablespoon dark soy sauce
- 1/2 tablespoon white vinegar
- 1 cup tuna flakes
- 1 tablespoon peanut oil
- 1 small onion, finely minced
- 1 cup cabbage, finely chopped
- 1 teaspoon garlic paste

Method

1. For dough, combine salt and flour in a bowl. Add in water gradually to make dough. Knead the dough into a bowl and set aside for half an hour.

2. For filling, combine all ingredients for filling and mix well.

3. Now. make 30 balls out of prepared dough and roll each one of them into 3 inches circle.

4. Then, place one of the rolled ball over a dim-sum mould and place 2 teaspoons of prepared filling in the centre. Apply some water at the edges and fold the mould into half to seal the dim-sum

5. Use the same method and rest of the dim-sums.

6. Line up a steam basket with cabbage leaves and place the prepared dim-sums in it. Then place the basket over boiling water and cook for 10-15 minutes or until done.

7. Serve hot with soy sauce!

Orange Jam Dim Sum

Dim Sums with orange jam filling!

Serves: 2

Preparation Time: 30 minutes

Cooking Time: 15 minutes

Ingredients

For Dough

- 1/8 teaspoon salt
- 1 1/2 cups flour
- water for kneading

For Filling

- 2 cups orange jam

Method

1. For dough, combine salt and flour in a bowl. Add in water gradually to make dough. Knead the dough into a bowl and set aside for half an hour.

2. Now. make 30 balls out of prepared dough and roll each one of them into 3 inches circle.

3. Then, place one of the rolled ball over a dim-sum mould and place 2 teaspoons of filling in the centre. Apply some water at the edges and fold the mould into half to seal the dim-sum

4. Use the same method and rest of the dim-sums.

5. Line up a steam basket with cabbage leaves and place the prepared dim-sums in it. Then place the basket over boiling water and cook for 10-15 minutes or until done.

6. Serve hot with soy sauce!

Jalapeno Cheese Dim Sum

Dim Sums with cream cheese and jalapeño!

Serves: 2

Preparation Time: 30 minutes

Cooking Time: 15 minutes

Ingredients

For Dough

- 1/8 teaspoon salt
- 1 1/2 cups flour
- water for kneading

For Filling

- 1/2 tablespoon dark soy sauce
- 1/2 tablespoon white vinegar
- 1/2 cup cream cheese
- 1/2 pickled jalapeños, finely chopped
- 1 tablespoon peanut oil
- 1 small onion, finely minced
- 1 cup cabbage, finely chopped
- 1 teaspoon garlic paste

Method

1. For dough, combine salt and flour in a bowl. Add in water gradually to make dough. Knead the dough into a bowl and set aside for half an hour.

2. For filling, combine all ingredients for filling and mix well.

3. Now. make 30 balls out of prepared dough and roll each one of them into 3 inches circle.

4. Then, place one of the rolled ball over a dim-sum mould and place 2 teaspoons of prepared filling in the centre. Apply some water at the edges and fold the mould into half to seal the dim-sum

5. Use the same method and rest of the dim-sums.

6. Line up a steam basket with cabbage leaves and place the prepared dim-sums in it. Then place the basket over boiling water and cook for 10-15 minutes or until done.

7. Serve hot with soy sauce!

Mozzarella Dim Sum

Dim Sums with mozzarella cheese and cabbage!

Serves: 2

Preparation Time: 30 minutes

Cooking Time: 15 minutes

Ingredients

For Dough

- 1/8 teaspoon salt
- 1 1/2 cups flour
- water for kneading

For Filling

- 1/2 tablespoon dark soy sauce
- 1/2 tablespoon white vinegar
- 1 cup mozzarella cheese, grated
- 1 tablespoon peanut oil
- 1 small onion, finely minced
- 1 cup cabbage, finely chopped
- 1 teaspoon garlic paste

Method

1. For dough, combine salt and flour in a bowl. Add in water gradually to make dough. Knead the dough into a bowl and set aside for half an hour.

2. For filling, combine all ingredients for filling and mix well.

3. Now. make 30 balls out of prepared dough and roll each one of them into 3 inches circle.

4. Then, place one of the rolled ball over a dim-sum mould and place 2 teaspoons of prepared filling in the centre. Apply some water at the edges and fold the mould into half to seal the dim-sum

5. Use the same method and rest of the dim-sums.

6. Line up a steam basket with cabbage leaves and place the prepared dim-sums in it. Then place the basket over boiling water and cook for 10-15 minutes or until done.

7. Serve hot with soy sauce!

Pumpkin Dim Sum

Dim Sums with pumpkin and cabbage!

Serves: 2

Preparation Time: 30 minutes

Cooking Time: 15 minutes

Ingredients

For Dough

- 1/8 teaspoon salt
- 1 1/2 cups flour
- water for kneading

For Filling

- 1/2 tablespoon dark soy sauce
- 1/2 tablespoon white vinegar
- 1 cup pumpkin, grated
- 1 tablespoon peanut oil
- 1 small onion, finely minced
- 1 cup cabbage, finely chopped
- 1 teaspoon garlic paste

Method

1. For dough, combine salt and flour in a bowl. Add in water gradually to make dough. Knead the dough into a bowl and set aside for half an hour.

1. For filling, combine all ingredients for filling and mix well.

2. Now. make 30 balls out of prepared dough and roll each one of them into 3 inches circle.

3. Then, place one of the rolled ball over a dim-sum mould and place 2 teaspoons of prepared filling in the centre. Apply some water at the edges and fold the mould into half to seal the dim-sum

4. Use the same method and rest of the dim-sums.

5. Line up a steam basket with cabbage leaves and place the prepared dim-sums in it. Then place the basket over boiling water and cook for 10-15 minutes or until done.

6. Serve hot with soy sauce!

Minced Chicken Dim Sum

Dim Sums with minced chicken and cabbage!

Serves: 2

Preparation Time: 30 minutes

Cooking Time: 15 minutes

Ingredients

For Dough

- 1/8 teaspoon salt
- 1 1/2 cups flour
- water for kneading

For Filling

- 1/2 tablespoon dark soy sauce
- 1/2 tablespoon white vinegar
- 1 cup minced chicken, minced
- 1 tablespoon peanut oil
- 1 small onion, finely minced
- 1 cup cabbage, finely chopped
- 1 teaspoon garlic paste

Method

1. For dough, combine salt and flour in a bowl. Add in water gradually to make dough. Knead the dough into a bowl and set aside for half an hour.

2. For filling, combine all ingredients for filling and mix well.

3. Now. make 30 balls out of prepared dough and roll each one of them into 3 inches circle.

4. Then, place one of the rolled ball over a dim-sum mould and place 2 teaspoons of prepared filling in the centre. Apply some water at the edges and fold the mould into half to seal the dim-sum

5. Use the same method and rest of the dim-sums.

6. Line up a steam basket with cabbage leaves and place the prepared dim-sums in it. Then place the basket over boiling water and cook for 10-15 minutes or until done.

7. Serve hot with soy sauce!

Salmon Dim Sum

Dim Sums with grilled salmon and cabbage!

Serves: 2

Preparation Time: 30 minutes

Cooking Time: 15 minutes

Ingredients

For Dough

- 1/8 teaspoon salt
- 1 1/2 cups flour
- water for kneading

For Filling

- 1/2 tablespoon dark soy sauce
- 1/2 tablespoon white vinegar
- 1 cup grilled salmon, shredded
- 1 tablespoon peanut oil
- 1 small onion, finely minced
- 1 cup cabbage, finely chopped
- 1 teaspoon garlic paste

Method

1. For dough, combine salt and flour in a bowl. Add in water gradually to make dough. Knead the dough into a bowl and set aside for half an hour.

2. For filling, combine all ingredients for filling and mix well.

3. Now. make 30 balls out of prepared dough and roll each one of them into 3 inches circle.

4. Then, place one of the rolled ball over a dim-sum mould and place 2 teaspoons of prepared filling in the centre. Apply some water at the edges and fold the mould into half to seal the dim-sum

5. Use the same method and rest of the dim-sums.

6. Line up a steam basket with cabbage leaves and place the prepared dim-sums in it. Then place the basket over boiling water and cook for 10-15 minutes or until done.

7. Serve hot with soy sauce!

Strawberry Dim Sum

Dim Sums with strawberry jam filling!

Serves: 2

Preparation Time: 30 minutes

Cooking Time: 15 minutes

Ingredients

For Dough

- 1/8 teaspoon salt
- 1 1/2 cups flour
- water for kneading

For Filling

- 2 cups strawberry jam

Method

1. For dough, combine salt and flour in a bowl. Add in water gradually to make dough. Knead the dough into a bowl and set aside for half an hour.

2. Now. make 30 balls out of prepared dough and roll each one of them into 3 inches circle.

3. Then, place one of the rolled ball over a dim-sum mould and place 2 teaspoons of filling in the centre. Apply some water at the edges and fold the mould into half to seal the dim-sum

4. Use the same method and rest of the dim-sums.

5. Line up a steam basket with cabbage leaves and place the prepared dim-sums in it. Then place the basket over boiling water and cook for 10-15 minutes or until done.

6. Serve hot with soy sauce!

Spaghetti Dim Sum

Dim Sums with left over spaghetti filling!

Serves: 2

Preparation Time: 30 minutes

Cooking Time: 15 minutes

Ingredients

For Dough

- 1/8 teaspoon salt
- 1 1/2 cups flour
- water for kneading

For Filling

- 2 cups left over spaghetti, finely chopped

Method

1. For dough, combine salt and flour in a bowl. Add in water gradually to make dough. Knead the dough into a bowl and set aside for half an hour.

2. Now. make 30 balls out of prepared dough and roll each one of them into 3 inches circle.

3. Then, place one of the rolled ball over a dim-sum mould and place 2 teaspoons of filling in the centre. Apply some water at the edges and fold the mould into half to seal the dim-sum

4. Use the same method and rest of the dim-sums.

5. Line up a steam basket with cabbage leaves and place the prepared dim-sums in it. Then place the basket over boiling water and cook for 10-15 minutes or until done.

6. Serve hot with soy sauce!

Cheddar Dim Sum

Dim Sums with cheddar cheese and cabbage!

Serves: 2

Preparation Time: 30 minutes

Cooking Time: 15 minutes

Ingredients

For Dough

- 1/8 teaspoon salt
- 1 1/2 cups flour
- water for kneading

For Filling

- 1/2 tablespoon dark soy sauce
- 1/2 tablespoon white vinegar
- 1 cup cheddar cheese, grated
- 1 tablespoon peanut oil
- 1 small onion, finely minced
- 1 cup cabbage, finely chopped
- 1 teaspoon garlic paste

Method

1. For dough, combine salt and flour in a bowl. Add in water gradually to make dough. Knead the dough into a bowl and set aside for half an hour.

2. For filling, combine all ingredients for filling and mix well.

3. Now. make 30 balls out of prepared dough and roll each one of them into 3 inches circle.

4. Then, place one of the rolled ball over a dim-sum mould and place 2 teaspoons of prepared filling in the centre. Apply some water at the edges and fold the mould into half to seal the dim-sum

5. Use the same method and rest of the dim-sums.

6. Line up a steam basket with cabbage leaves and place the prepared dim-sums in it. Then place the basket over boiling water and cook for 10-15 minutes or until done.

7. Serve hot with soy sauce!

Hummus Onion Dim Sum

Dim Sums with humus and onion!

Serves: 2

Preparation Time: 30 minutes

Cooking Time: 15 minutes

Ingredients

For Dough

- 1/8 teaspoon salt
- 1 1/2 cups flour
- water for kneading

For Filling

- 1/2 tablespoon dark soy sauce
- 1/2 tablespoon white vinegar
- 1 cup humus
- 1 tablespoon peanut oil
- 1 small onion, finely minced
- 1 cup cabbage, finely chopped
- 1 teaspoon garlic paste

Method

1. For dough, combine salt and flour in a bowl. Add in water gradually to make dough. Knead the dough into a bowl and set aside for half an hour.

2. For filling, combine all ingredients for filling and mix well.

3. Now. make 30 balls out of prepared dough and roll each one of them into 3 inches circle.

4. Then, place one of the rolled ball over a dim-sum mould and place 2 teaspoons of prepared filling in the centre. Apply some water at the edges and fold the mould into half to seal the dim-sum

5. Use the same method and rest of the dim-sums.

6. Line up a steam basket with cabbage leaves and place the prepared dim-sums in it. Then place the basket over boiling water and cook for 10-15 minutes or until done.

7. Serve hot with soy sauce!

Broccoli Dim Sum

Dim Sums with broccoli and cabbage!

Serves: 2

Preparation Time: 30 minutes

Cooking Time: 15 minutes

Ingredients

For Dough

- 1/8 teaspoon salt
- 1 1/2 cups flour
- water for kneading

For Filling

- 1/2 tablespoon dark soy sauce
- 1/2 tablespoon white vinegar
- 1 cup broccoli, grated
- 1 tablespoon peanut oil
- 1 small onion, finely minced
- 1 cup cabbage, finely chopped
- 1 teaspoon garlic paste

Method

1. For dough, combine salt and flour in a bowl. Add in water gradually to make dough. Knead the dough into a bowl and set aside for half an hour.

2. For filling, combine all ingredients for filling and mix well.

3. Now. make 30 balls out of prepared dough and roll each one of them into 3 inches circle.

4. Then, place one of the rolled ball over a dim-sum mould and place 2 teaspoons of prepared filling in the centre. Apply some water at the edges and fold the mould into half to seal the dim-sum

5. Use the same method and rest of the dim-sums.

6. Line up a steam basket with cabbage leaves and place the prepared dim-sums in it. Then place the basket over boiling water and cook for 10-15 minutes or until done.

7. Serve hot with soy sauce!

Raspberry Dim Sum

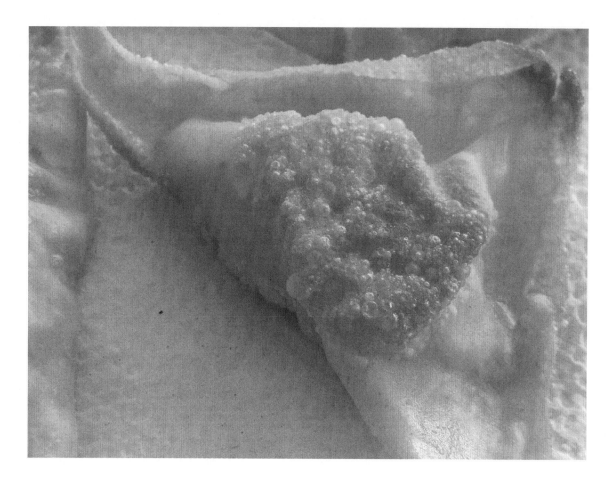

Dim Sums with raspberry jam filling!

Serves: 2

Preparation Time: 30 minutes

Cooking Time: 15 minutes

Ingredients

For Dough

- 1/8 teaspoon salt
- 1 1/2 cups flour
- water for kneading

For Filling

- 2 cups raspberry jam

Method

1. For dough, combine salt and flour in a bowl. Add in water gradually to make dough. Knead the dough into a bowl and set aside for half an hour.

2. Now. make 30 balls out of prepared dough and roll each one of them into 3 inches circle.

3. Then, place one of the rolled ball over a dim-sum mould and place 2 teaspoons of filling in the centre. Apply some water at the edges and fold the mould into half to seal the dim-sum

4. Use the same method and rest of the dim-sums.

5. Line up a steam basket with cabbage leaves and place the prepared dim-sums in it. Then place the basket over boiling water and cook for 10-15 minutes or until done.

6. Serve hot with soy sauce!

Ricotta Oregano

Dim Sums with ricotta cheese and cabbage!

Serves: 2

Preparation Time: 30 minutes

Cooking Time: 15 minutes

Ingredients

For Dough

- 1/8 teaspoon salt
- 1 1/2 cups flour
- water for kneading

For Filling

- 1/2 tablespoon dark soy sauce
- 1/2 tablespoon white vinegar
- 1 cup ricotta cheese, crumpled
- 1 tablespoon peanut oil
- 1 small onion, finely minced
- 1 cup cabbage, finely chopped
- 1 teaspoon garlic paste

Method

1. For dough, combine salt and flour in a bowl. Add in water gradually to make dough. Knead the dough into a bowl and set aside for half an hour.

2. For filling, combine all ingredients for filling and mix well.

3. Now. make 30 balls out of prepared dough and roll each one of them into 3 inches circle.

4. Then, place one of the rolled ball over a dim-sum mould and place 2 teaspoons of prepared filling in the centre. Apply some water at the edges and fold the mould into half to seal the dim-sum

5. Use the same method and rest of the dim-sums.

6. Line up a steam basket with cabbage leaves and place the prepared dim-sums in it. Then place the basket over boiling water and cook for 10-15 minutes or until done.

7. Serve hot with soy sauce!

Cheese Dim Sum

Dim Sums with mozzarella and cheddar cheese!

Serves: 2

Preparation Time: 30 minutes

Cooking Time: 15 minutes

Ingredients

For Dough

- 1/8 teaspoon salt
- 1 1/2 cups flour
- water for kneading

For Filling

- 1/2 tablespoon dark soy sauce
- 1/2 tablespoon white vinegar
- 1/2 cup mozzarella cheese, shredded
- 1/2 cup cheddar cheese, shredded
- 1 tablespoon peanut oil
- 1 small onion, finely minced
- 1 cup cabbage, finely chopped
- 1 teaspoon garlic paste

Method

1. For dough, combine salt and flour in a bowl. Add in water gradually to make dough. Knead the dough into a bowl and set aside for half an hour.

2. For filling, combine all ingredients for filling and mix well.

3. Now. make 30 balls out of prepared dough and roll each one of them into 3 inches circle.

4. Then, place one of the rolled ball over a dim-sum mould and place 2 teaspoons of prepared filling in the centre. Apply some water at the edges and fold the mould into half to seal the dim-sum

5. Use the same method and rest of the dim-sums.

6. Line up a steam basket with cabbage leaves and place the prepared dim-sums in it. Then place the basket over boiling water and cook for 10-15 minutes or until done.

7. Serve hot with soy sauce!

Duck Dim Sum

Dim Sums with minced duck breast and cabbage!

Serves: 2

Preparation Time: 30 minutes

Cooking Time: 15 minutes

Ingredients

For Dough

- 1/8 teaspoon salt
- 1 1/2 cups flour
- water for kneading

For Filling

- 1/2 tablespoon dark soy sauce
- 1/2 tablespoon white vinegar
- 1 cup duck breast, minced
- 1 tablespoon peanut oil
- 1 small onion, finely minced
- 1 cup cabbage, finely chopped
- 1 teaspoon garlic paste

Method

1. For dough, combine salt and flour in a bowl. Add in water gradually to make dough. Knead the dough into a bowl and set aside for half an hour.

2. For filling, combine all ingredients for filling and mix well.

3. Now. make 30 balls out of prepared dough and roll each one of them into 3 inches circle.

4. Then, place one of the rolled ball over a dim-sum mould and place 2 teaspoons of prepared filling in the centre. Apply some water at the edges and fold the mould into half to seal the dim-sum

5. Use the same method and rest of the dim-sums.

6. Line up a steam basket with cabbage leaves and place the prepared dim-sums in it. Then place the basket over boiling water and cook for 10-15 minutes or until done.

7. Serve hot with soy sauce!

Cream Cheese Olive Dim Sum

Dim Sums with black olives and cream cheese!

Serves: 2

Preparation Time: 30 minutes

Cooking Time: 15 minutes

Ingredients

For Dough

- 1/8 teaspoon salt
- 1 1/2 cups flour
- water for kneading

For Filling

- 1/2 tablespoon dark soy sauce
- 1/2 tablespoon white vinegar
- 1/2 cup cream cheese
- 1/2 cup black olives, finely chopped
- 1 tablespoon peanut oil
- 1 small onion, finely minced
- 1 cup cabbage, finely chopped
- 1 teaspoon garlic paste

Method

1. For dough, combine salt and flour in a bowl. Add in water gradually to make dough. Knead the dough into a bowl and set aside for half an hour.

2. For filling, combine all ingredients for filling and mix well.

3. Now. make 30 balls out of prepared dough and roll each one of them into 3 inches circle.

4. Then, place one of the rolled ball over a dim-sum mould and place 2 teaspoons of prepared filling in the centre. Apply some water at the edges and fold the mould into half to seal the dim-sum

5. Use the same method and rest of the dim-sums.

6. Line up a steam basket with cabbage leaves and place the prepared dim-sums in it. Then place the basket over boiling water and cook for 10-15 minutes or until done.

7. Serve hot with soy sauce!

Peach Dim Sum

Dim Sums with peach jam filling!

Serves: 2

Preparation Time: 30 minutes

Cooking Time: 15 minutes

Ingredients

For Dough

- 1/8 teaspoon salt
- 1 1/2 cups flour
- water for kneading

For Filling

- 2 cups Peach jam

Method

1. For dough, combine salt and flour in a bowl. Add in water gradually to make dough. Knead the dough into a bowl and set aside for half an hour.

2. Now. make 30 balls out of prepared dough and roll each one of them into 3 inches circle.

3. Then, place one of the rolled ball over a dim-sum mould and place 2 teaspoons of filling in the centre. Apply some water at the edges and fold the mould into half to seal the dim-sum

4. Use the same method and rest of the dim-sums.

5. Line up a steam basket with cabbage leaves and place the prepared dim-sums in it. Then place the basket over boiling water and cook for 10-15 minutes or until done.

6. Serve hot with soy sauce!

Walnut Caramel Dim Sum

Dim Sums with walnuts and caramel!

Serves: 2

Preparation Time: 30 minutes

Cooking Time: 15 minutes

Ingredients

For Dough

- 1/8 teaspoon salt
- 1 1/2 cups flour
- water for kneading

For Filling

- 1/2 cup caramel
- 1 1/2 cups walnuts, finely chopped

Method

1. For dough, combine salt and flour in a bowl. Add in water gradually to make dough. Knead the dough into a bowl and set aside for half an hour.

2. For filling, combine all ingredients for filling and mix well.

3. Now. make 30 balls out of prepared dough and roll each one of them into 3 inches circle.

4. Then, place one of the rolled ball over a dim-sum mould and place 2 teaspoons of prepared filling in the centre. Apply some water at the edges and fold the mould into half to seal the dim-sum

5. Use the same method and rest of the dim-sums.

6. Line up a steam basket with cabbage leaves and place the prepared dim-sums in it. Then place the basket over boiling water and cook for 10-15 minutes or until done.

7. Serve hot with soy sauce!

Chorizo Dim Sum

Dim Sums with chorizo and onion!

Serves: 2

Preparation Time: 30 minutes

Cooking Time: 15 minutes

Ingredients

For Dough

- 1/8 teaspoon salt
- 1 1/2 cups flour
- water for kneading

For Filling

- 1/2 tablespoon dark soy sauce
- 1/2 tablespoon white vinegar
- 1 cup chorizo, crumpled
- 1 tablespoon peanut oil
- 1 small onion, finely minced
- 1 cup cabbage, finely chopped
- 1 teaspoon garlic paste

Method

1. For dough, combine salt and flour in a bowl. Add in water gradually to make dough. Knead the dough into a bowl and set aside for half an hour.

2. For filling, combine all ingredients for filling and mix well.

3. Now. make 30 balls out of prepared dough and roll each one of them into 3 inches circle.

4. Then, place one of the rolled ball over a dim-sum mould and place 2 teaspoons of prepared filling in the centre. Apply some water at the edges and fold the mould into half to seal the dim-sum

5. Use the same method and rest of the dim-sums.

6. Line up a steam basket with cabbage leaves and place the prepared dim-sums in it. Then place the basket over boiling water and cook for 10-15 minutes or until done.

7. Serve hot with soy sauce!

Gouda Basil Dim Sum

Dim Sums with gouda cheese and cabbage!

Serves: 2

Preparation Time: 30 minutes

Cooking Time: 15 minutes

Ingredients

For Dough

- 1/8 teaspoon salt
- 1 1/2 cups flour
- water for kneading

For Filling

- 1/2 tablespoon dark soy sauce
- 1/2 tablespoon white vinegar
- 1 cup gouda cheese, grated
- 1 tablespoon peanut oil
- 1 small onion, finely minced
- 1 cup cabbage, finely chopped
- 1 teaspoon garlic paste

Method

1. For dough, combine salt and flour in a bowl. Add in water gradually to make dough. Knead the dough into a bowl and set aside for half an hour.

2. For filling, combine all ingredients for filling and mix well.

3. Now. make 30 balls out of prepared dough and roll each one of them into 3 inches circle.

4. Then, place one of the rolled ball over a dim-sum mould and place 2 teaspoons of prepared filling in the centre. Apply some water at the edges and fold the mould into half to seal the dim-sum

5. Use the same method and rest of the dim-sums.

6. Line up a steam basket with cabbage leaves and place the prepared dim-sums in it. Then place the basket over boiling water and cook for 10-15 minutes or until done.

7. Serve hot with soy sauce!

Blackberry Dim Sum

Dim Sums with blackberry jam filling!

Serves: 2

Preparation Time: 30 minutes

Cooking Time: 15 minutes

Ingredients

For Dough

- 1/8 teaspoon salt
- 1 1/2 cups flour
- water for kneading

For Filling

- 2 cups blackberry jam

Method

1. For dough, combine salt and flour in a bowl. Add in water gradually to make dough. Knead the dough into a bowl and set aside for half an hour.

2. Now. make 30 balls out of prepared dough and roll each one of them into 3 inches circle.

3. Then, place one of the rolled ball over a dim-sum mould and place 2 teaspoons of filling in the centre. Apply some water at the edges and fold the mould into half to seal the dim-sum

4. Use the same method and rest of the dim-sums.

5. Line up a steam basket with cabbage leaves and place the prepared dim-sums in it. Then place the basket over boiling water and cook for 10-15 minutes or until done.

6. Serve hot with soy sauce!

Parmesan Parsley Dim Sum

Dim Sums with parmesan cheese and parsley leaves!

Serves: 2

Preparation Time: 30 minutes

Cooking Time: 15 minutes

Ingredients

For Dough

- 1/8 teaspoon salt
- 1 1/2 cups flour
- water for kneading

For Filling

- 1/2 tablespoon dark soy sauce
- 1/2 tablespoon white vinegar
- 1/2 cup fresh parsley leaves, nicely chopped
- 1/2 cup parmesan cheese, grated
- 1 tablespoon peanut oil
- 1 small onion, finely minced
- 1 cup cabbage, finely chopped
- 1 teaspoon garlic paste

Method

1. For dough, combine salt and flour in a bowl. Add in water gradually to make dough. Knead the dough into a bowl and set aside for half an hour.

2. For filling, combine all ingredients for filling and mix well.

3. Now. make 30 balls out of prepared dough and roll each one of them into 3 inches circle.

4. Then, place one of the rolled ball over a dim-sum mould and place 2 teaspoons of prepared filling in the centre. Apply some water at the edges and fold the mould into half to seal the dim-sum

5. Use the same method and rest of the dim-sums.

6. Line up a steam basket with cabbage leaves and place the prepared dim-sums in it. Then place the basket over boiling water and cook for 10-15 minutes or until done.

7. Serve hot with soy sauce!

Tofu Bell Pepper Dim Sum

Dim Sums with tofu and bell pepper!

Serves: 2

Preparation Time: 30 minutes

Cooking Time: 15 minutes

Ingredients

For Dough

- 1/8 teaspoon salt
- 1 1/2 cups flour
- water for kneading

For Filling

- 1/2 tablespoon dark soy sauce
- 1/2 tablespoon white vinegar
- 1 cup firm tofu, finely chopped
- 1 tablespoon peanut oil
- 1 small onion, finely minced
- 1 cup green bell pepper, finely chopped
- 1 teaspoon garlic paste

Method

1. For dough, combine salt and flour in a bowl. Add in water gradually to make dough. Knead the dough into a bowl and set aside for half an hour.

2. For filling, combine all ingredients for filling and mix well.

3. Now. make 30 balls out of prepared dough and roll each one of them into 3 inches circle.

4. Then, place one of the rolled ball over a dim-sum mould and place 2 teaspoons of prepared filling in the centre. Apply some water at the edges and fold the mould into half to seal the dim-sum

5. Use the same method and rest of the dim-sums.

6. Line up a steam basket with cabbage leaves and place the prepared dim-sums in it. Then place the basket over boiling water and cook for 10-15 minutes or until done.

7. Serve hot with soy sauce!

Mix Fruit Jam Dim Sum

Dim Sums with mixed fruit jam filling!

Serves: 2

Preparation Time: 30 minutes

Cooking Time: 15 minutes

Ingredients

For Dough

- 1/8 teaspoon salt
- 1 1/2 cups flour
- water for kneading

For Filling

- 2 cups Mixed fruit jam

Method

1. For dough, combine salt and flour in a bowl. Add in water gradually to make dough. Knead the dough into a bowl and set aside for half an hour.

2. Now. make 30 balls out of prepared dough and roll each one of them into 3 inches circle.

3. Then, place one of the rolled ball over a dim-sum mould and place 2 teaspoons of filling in the centre. Apply some water at the edges and fold the mould into half to seal the dim-sum

4. Use the same method and rest of the dim-sums.

5. Line up a steam basket with cabbage leaves and place the prepared dim-sums in it. Then place the basket over boiling water and cook for 10-15 minutes or until done.

6. Serve hot with soy sauce!

Ham Goat Cheese Dim Sum

Dim Sums with ham and goat cheese!

Serves: 2

Preparation Time: 30 minutes

Cooking Time: 15 minutes

Ingredients

For Dough

- 1/8 teaspoon salt
- 1 1/2 cups flour
- water for kneading

For Filling

- 1/2 tablespoon dark soy sauce
- 1/2 tablespoon white vinegar
- 1/2 cup ham, finely chopped
- 1/2 cup goat cheese, grated
- 1 tablespoon peanut oil
- 1 small onion, finely minced
- 1 cup cabbage, finely chopped
- 1 teaspoon garlic paste

Method

1. For dough, combine salt and flour in a bowl. Add in water gradually to make dough. Knead the dough into a bowl and set aside for half an hour.

2. For filling, combine all ingredients for filling and mix well.

3. Now. make 30 balls out of prepared dough and roll each one of them into 3 inches circle.

4. Then, place one of the rolled ball over a dim-sum mould and place 2 teaspoons of prepared filling in the centre. Apply some water at the edges and fold the mould into half to seal the dim-sum

5. Use the same method and rest of the dim-sums.

6. Line up a steam basket with cabbage leaves and place the prepared dim-sums in it. Then place the basket over boiling water and cook for 10-15 minutes or until done.

7. Serve hot with soy sauce!

Hotdog Dim Sum

Dim Sums with sausage and mustard sauce!

Serves: 2

Preparation Time: 30 minutes

Cooking Time: 15 minutes

Ingredients

For Dough

- 1/8 teaspoon salt
- 1 1/2 cups flour
- water for kneading

For Filling

- 1/2 tablespoon dark soy sauce
- 1/2 tablespoon white vinegar
- 1 cup sausage, finely chopped
- 1 tablespoon mustard sauce
- 1 tablespoon peanut oil
- 1 small onion, finely minced
- 1 cup cabbage, finely chopped
- 1 teaspoon garlic paste

Method

1. For dough, combine salt and flour in a bowl. Add in water gradually to make dough. Knead the dough into a bowl and set aside for half an hour.

2. For filling, combine all ingredients for filling and mix well.

3. Now. make 30 balls out of prepared dough and roll each one of them into 3 inches circle.

4. Then, place one of the rolled ball over a dim-sum mould and place 2 teaspoons of prepared filling in the centre. Apply some water at the edges and fold the mould into half to seal the dim-sum

5. Use the same method and rest of the dim-sums.

6. Line up a steam basket with cabbage leaves and place the prepared dim-sums in it. Then place the basket over boiling water and cook for 10-15 minutes or until done.

7. Serve hot with soy sauce!

Salami Mayo Dim Sum

Dim Sums with salami and mayo!

Serves: 2

Preparation Time: 30 minutes

Cooking Time: 15 minutes

Ingredients

For Dough

- 1/8 teaspoon salt
- 1 1/2 cups flour
- water for kneading

For Filling

- 1/2 tablespoon dark soy sauce
- 1/2 tablespoon white vinegar
- 1 cup salami, finely chopped
- 2 tablespoons mayo
- 1 small onion, finely minced
- 1 cup cabbage, finely chopped
- 1 teaspoon garlic paste

Method

1. For dough, combine salt and flour in a bowl. Add in water gradually to make dough. Knead the dough into a bowl and set aside for half an hour.

2. For filling, combine all ingredients for filling and mix well.

3. Now. make 30 balls out of prepared dough and roll each one of them into 3 inches circle.

4. Then, place one of the rolled ball over a dim-sum mould and place 2 teaspoons of prepared filling in the centre. Apply some water at the edges and fold the mould into half to seal the dim-sum

5. Use the same method and rest of the dim-sums.

6. Line up a steam basket with cabbage leaves and place the prepared dim-sums in it. Then place the basket over boiling water and cook for 10-15 minutes or until done.

7. Serve hot with soy sauce!

Smoked Cheese Paprika Dim Sum

Dim Sums with smoked cheese and paprika!

Serves: 2

Preparation Time: 30 minutes

Cooking Time: 15 minutes

Ingredients

For Dough

- 1/8 teaspoon salt
- 1 1/2 cups flour
- water for kneading

For Filling

- 1/2 tablespoon dark soy sauce
- 1/2 tablespoon white vinegar
- 1 cup smoked cheese, grated
- 2 teaspoons paprika
- 1 tablespoon peanut oil
- 1 small onion, finely minced
- 1 cup cabbage, finely chopped
- 1 teaspoon garlic paste

Method

1. For dough, combine salt and flour in a bowl. Add in water gradually to make dough. Knead the dough into a bowl and set aside for half an hour.

2. For filling, combine all ingredients for filling and mix well.

3. Now. make 30 balls out of prepared dough and roll each one of them into 3 inches circle.

4. Then, place one of the rolled ball over a dim-sum mould and place 2 teaspoons of prepared filling in the centre. Apply some water at the edges and fold the mould into half to seal the dim-sum

5. Use the same method and rest of the dim-sums.

6. Line up a steam basket with cabbage leaves and place the prepared dim-sums in it. Then place the basket over boiling water and cook for 10-15 minutes or until done.

7. Serve hot with soy sauce!

Minced Pork Dim Sum

Dim Sums with minced pork and cabbage!

Serves: 2

Preparation Time: 30 minutes

Cooking Time: 15 minutes

Ingredients

For Dough

- 1/8 teaspoon salt
- 1 1/2 cups flour
- water for kneading

For Filling

- 1/2 tablespoon dark soy sauce
- 1/2 tablespoon white vinegar
- 1 cup pork loin, minced
- 1 tablespoon peanut oil
- 1 small onion, finely minced
- 1 cup cabbage, finely chopped
- 1 teaspoon garlic paste

Method

1. For dough, combine salt and flour in a bowl. Add in water gradually to make dough. Knead the dough into a bowl and set aside for half an hour.

2. For filling, combine all ingredients for filling and mix well.

3. Now. make 30 balls out of prepared dough and roll each one of them into 3 inches circle.

4. Then, place one of the rolled ball over a dim-sum mould and place 2 teaspoons of prepared filling in the centre. Apply some water at the edges and fold the mould into half to seal the dim-sum

5. Use the same method and rest of the dim-sums.

6. Line up a steam basket with cabbage leaves and place the prepared dim-sums in it. Then place the basket over boiling water and cook for 10-15 minutes or until done.

7. Serve hot with soy sauce!

Mango Dim Sum

Dim Sums with mango jam filling!

Serves: 2

Preparation Time: 30 minutes

Cooking Time: 15 minutes

Ingredients

For Dough

- 1/8 teaspoon salt
- 1 1/2 cups flour
- water for kneading

For Filling

- 2 cups mango jam

Method

1. For dough, combine salt and flour in a bowl. Add in water gradually to make dough. Knead the dough into a bowl and set aside for half an hour.

2. Now. make 30 balls out of prepared dough and roll each one of them into 3 inches circle.

3. Then, place one of the rolled ball over a dim-sum mould and place 2 teaspoons of filling in the centre. Apply some water at the edges and fold the mould into half to seal the dim-sum

4. Use the same method and rest of the dim-sums.

5. Line up a steam basket with cabbage leaves and place the prepared dim-sums in it. Then place the basket over boiling water and cook for 10-15 minutes or until done.

6. Serve hot with soy sauce!

Conclusion

In China, "Dim Sum" signifies "touch the heart," and through this recipe book, we have tried to do the same. 50 carefully explained, unique recipes so that each one of you can easily re-create these delightful morsels.

Anybody who would love to have a dim-sum meal must have imagined what it would be like to prepare these tasty little packs at home. The answer, unexpectedly, is simple to cook. Organize a tea or lunch or dinner menu and make these delicious dim-sums from this irresistible collection of recipes.

About the Author

Ivy's mission is to share her recipes with the world. Even though she is not a professional cook she has always had that flair toward cooking. Her hands create magic. She can make even the simplest recipe tastes superb. Everyone who has tried her food has astounding their compliments was what made her think about writing recipes.

She wanted everyone to have a taste of her creations aside from close family and friends. So, deciding to write recipes was her winning decision. She isn't interested in popularity, but how many people have her recipes reached and touched people. Each recipe in her cookbooks is special and has a special meaning in her life. This means that each recipe is created with attention and love. Every ingredient carefully picked, every combination tried and tested.

Her mission started on her birthday about 9 years ago, when her guests couldn't stop prizing the food on the table. The next thing she did was organizing an event where chefs from restaurants were tasting her recipes. This event gave her the courage to start spreading her recipes.

She has written many cookbooks and she is still working on more. There is no end in the art of cooking; all you need is inspiration, love, and dedication.

Author's Afterthoughts

I am thankful for downloading this book and taking the time to read it. I know that you have learned a lot and you had a great time reading it. Writing books is the best way to share the skills I have with your and the best tips too.

I know that there are many books and choosing my book is amazing. I am thankful that you stopped and took time to decide. You made a great decision and I am sure that you enjoyed it.

I will be even happier if you provide honest feedback about my book. Feedbacks helped by growing and they still do. They help me to choose better content and new ideas. So, maybe your feedback can trigger an idea for my next book.

Thank you again

Sincerely

Ivy Hope

Printed in Great Britain
by Amazon